THE MAGICAL HISTORY OF
Mermaids

Publisher and Creative Director: Nick Wells
Senior Project Editor: Catherine Taylor
Art Director & Layout Design: Mike Spender
Digital Design & Production: Chris Herbert
Copy Editor: Anna Groves
Proofreader: Dawn Laker

Special thanks to: Frances Bodiam, George Nash
and the artists who allowed us to reproduce their work

FLAME TREE PUBLISHING

6 Melbray Mews, Fulham,
London SW6 3NS, United Kingdom
www.flametreepublishing.com

First published 2018

© 2018 Flame Tree Publishing Ltd

(Artwork © respective contributors – *see* page 127)

18 20 22 21 19
1 3 5 7 9 10 8 6 4 2

ISBN 978-1-78664-793-1

A CIP record for this book is available from the British Library upon request.

Printed in China

THE MAGICAL HISTORY OF
Mermaids

Russ Thorne

FOREWORD BY TERA LYNN CHILDS

FLAME TREE
PUBLISHING

CONTENTS

FOREWORD

I can't remember a time when I didn't want to be a mermaid. I have always been drawn to the sense of freedom, to the dream of going wherever the water leads, exploring breathtaking worlds unseen by human eyes, and swimming alongside dolphins, seals and schools of rainbow-coloured fish.

I'm not sure where this fascination began. Maybe when I saw the movie *Splash*. I was eight years old and I wanted to be Madison so badly. My cousin and I spent most of that summer throwing water on each other, hoping we would suddenly sprout fins.

As I got older, I wanted to spend as much time in the water as possible. So I became a competitive swimmer. One memory from that time is particularly vivid.

It was after a summer practice in the outdoor pool. My hair was long and bleached blond by sun and chlorine. Everyone else had left the water, so I swam down to the bottom and twisted myself around to face the surface. As my hair swirled around me and the sunlight glittered through the water, it was as close to becoming a mermaid as I have ever felt.

The search for that feeling has never left me, which possibly explains why, many years later, on a quiet beach on the Florida Gulf Coast, I found my mind wandering to the mer world. As I stared out over the rippling water, I thought, *I wish a merman would emerge from the ocean and bestow his magical powers on me with a kiss.*

My merman never appeared, but that momentary fantasy eventually morphed into the *Forgive My Fins* series. With those books, I hope I have passed on a love of mermaids to new generations. As will this book, I am sure.

And maybe, if the mermaids appreciate my efforts to share them with the world, one day they'll make my wish come true.

TERA LYNN CHILDS

teralynnchilds.com

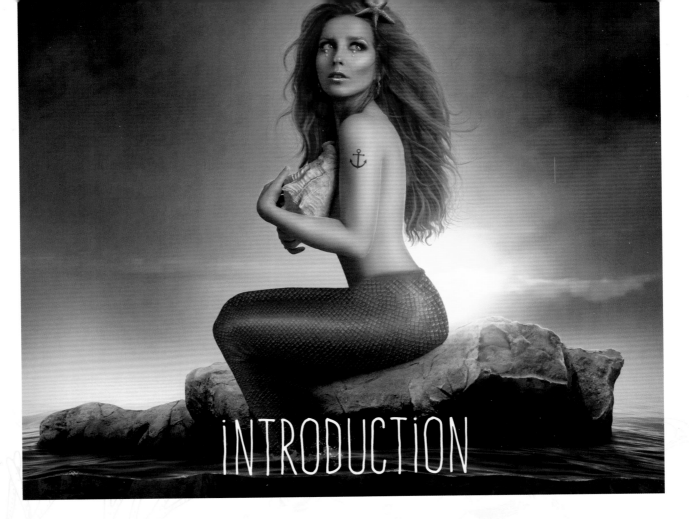

iNTRODUCTiON

Mermaids. They're everywhere. Looking around at the t-shirts, dolls, cartoons, bath toys, stationery, speciality coffee and other mermaid-themed jumble that you can find pretty much anywhere now, it would be easy to think that mermaids are a new-fangled fashion that just arrived. Far from it.

Mermaids are basically as old as humanity. Since the earliest humans stood by the sea and whispered 'wow' to one another, we've told mermaid stories. That's part of who we are: we live on a watery world, surrounded by extraordinary oceans teeming with extraordinary life, and we're natural storytellers.

Love, Fear and Folklore

We've created fabulous beings – dragons, unicorns, giants, gods, monsters – since forever. Stories about them entertain us, but they also help us make sense of the world. Ancient civilizations struggled to understand the vast power of the sea or the storms, so the waves and skies became the home of supernatural beings and terrible creatures who made it all happen.

I was a mermaid in my past life. I just feel it when I go in the sea. I just feel a connection there between me, and the water …

ELLA HENDERSON

Mermaids fit right into that. We love and fear them just as we love and fear the sea, and they're endlessly mysterious to us, just as the deepest silent depths of the oceans are. We'll never fully understand mermaids or their watery realm, but that won't stop us exploring. That's what this book is here for.

9

MEET THE MERMAIDS

The first thing to understand about the mermaid is that she's as changeable, beautiful and terrible as the tide. Over the centuries, there have been countless mermaid myths, and the mermaid means different things to different cultures. Still, we have to start somewhere, and the name is as good a place to dive in as any.

What's in a Name?

Our modern word 'mermaid' is a blend of the Old English word 'mere' (from the Germanic 'Meer' – 'sea') and the Middle English 'maid' (girl, or young woman). Celtic mermaids were known as 'merrow', which again means 'sea maid'; in Latvia, they're called 'nara'. So many names, but they generally describe a female water-dwelling

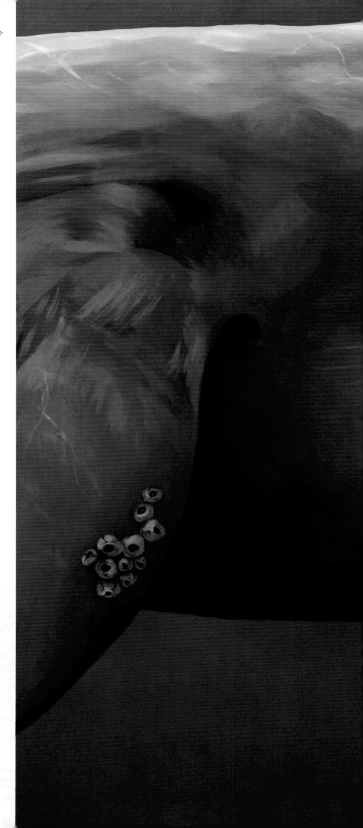

spirit, usually with magical powers. However, the waters of humanity have been packed with all kinds of deities across history, so we'll need to focus in a bit.

Mermaids are usually corporeal – as in flesh and blood – as opposed to other spirits like water nymphs and naiads. They're different to selkies, shapeshifters who also live in the water but wear a kind of magical sealskin. These and other divine water spirits deserve an honourable mention here, but our focus is on mermaids. The same goes for mermen: there's plenty to say about Triton and other mer-chaps, but it's the ladies who have really captured our collective imaginations.

She had long hair, from which the water dripped, hanging straight on either side of her little face; but it was green hair, something like the seaweed which clothed the rock, only finer and prettier.

NETTA SYRETT, A SEA CHILD

Appearance

This might seem like an easy one: mermaids are the beautiful ones with the fish tails. Well, yes, but within that description there's plenty of wriggle room. The 'classic' European mermaid look only really arrived in the last few hundred years, made popular in part thanks to Hans Christian Andersen's *The Little Mermaid* (1836) and the paintings of Victorian artists. She has long flowing hair that she combs with shells, a naked torso and the lower half of a fish.

However, exactly how much of her is fish varies a lot. Some artists or writers have her as fish from the waist down; others have the tail starting below the knees. There's even disagreement on whether or not she's beautiful: to some she's demonic, or animal-like; to others, she's female beauty perfected.

> *I must be a mermaid …*
> *I have no fear of depths*
> *and a great fear of*
> *shallow living.*
>
> ANAÏS NIN

Symbolism

As aquatic beings, mermaids come draped in all the different things the sea means to us. They can symbolize its fury, but also its beauty; its excitement and allure, but also its loneliness and danger. A mermaid is a complicated being; she's all of those things in one package.

Mermaids also represent feminine power and mystery, and their close association with water – the stuff of life itself – makes them powerful symbols of birth and fertility. Some people even suggest that mermaids remind us that we're animals but also different to animals – we all carry that part-human, part-animal contrast within us, and mermaids personify this.

Mermaid Powers

As magical beings, mermaids have a lot of different powers. Some myths tell us that they can summon the waves and conjure storms, or calm seas, depending on their mood. They can communicate with the creatures of the deep, and can bewitch people (often men) with their singing, but they can also be compassionate, helping those in peril on the sea by pulling them from the waves or warning of danger ahead.

Mermaids are big-hearted and tend to fall in love a lot, if the stories are to be believed. Unfortunately, this doesn't always end well, as being grabbed and dragged under the sea isn't everyone's idea of romance, but it does show that mermaids are loving souls, even if they have a funny way of showing it.

Where Do Mermaids Come From?

Because water and water spirits have always been important to civilizations both ancient and modern, there's bound to be a part of us that still feels that connection, which might explain why mermaids are still so appealing. But there are a few solid possibilities for where it all began, including the super-rare medical condition sirenomelia – also known as 'mermaid syndrome' – in which people are born with their legs fused together. It's possible that early cases of sirenomelia were behind some of the first descriptions of mermaids, but of course we'll never know for sure.

Whether the mermaid sprang from the human imagination or a medical anomaly, once the idea of her was in place, the myth machine could really run wild – as we'll see in the next chapter.

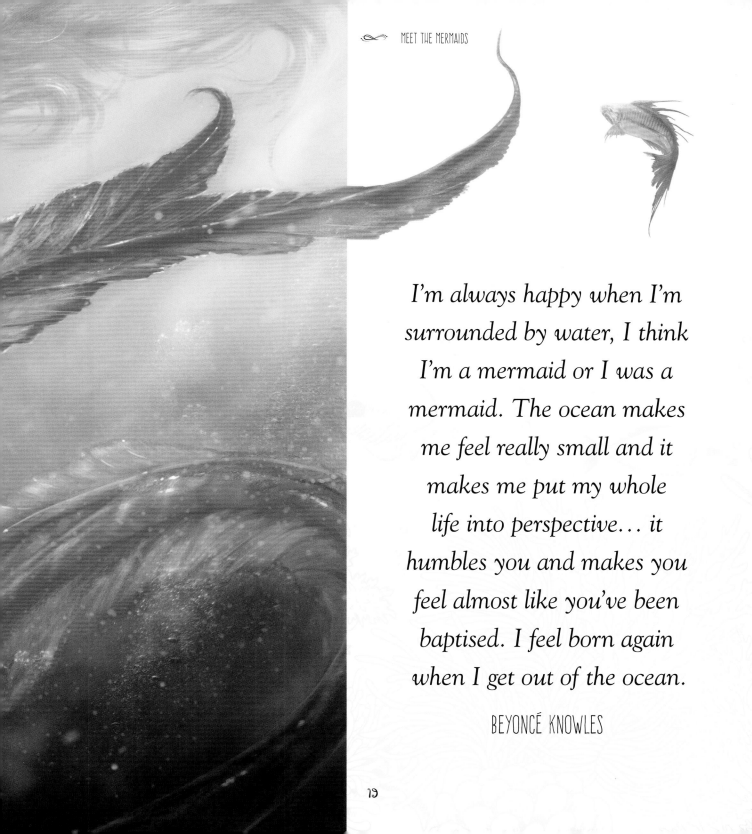

I'm always happy when I'm surrounded by water, I think I'm a mermaid or I was a mermaid. The ocean makes me feel really small and it makes me put my whole life into perspective… it humbles you and makes you feel almost like you've been baptised. I feel born again when I get out of the ocean.

BEYONCÉ KNOWLES

THE FIRST MERMAIDS

f we want to understand how mermaids have come to be such an important part of our culture, we need to start by taking a walk (or perhaps a swim) through the ancient world. The earliest human civilizations saw gods and magic everywhere, with divine beings living on the highest mountains and in the darkest caves and deepest jungles. Water was essential for survival and early humans would never live far from it, so almost every river and ocean had its own divine being. Sounds like just the sort of place to conjure up mermaids.

Fanciful Fish

Mermaid-like beings pop up in human culture in the Old Babylonian period

(around 1830 BC) in Mesopotamia – the part of the world that's now Iraq and Kuwait. They don't arrive as fully formed beautiful maidens, however. Early Mesopotamian art features beings that are part-human, part-fish and usually male, although some female versions do exist. According to some scholars, these female beings were called *kuliltu*, or 'fish women'.

I think every little girl's dream is to be a mermaid or to see a mermaid. [When I was younger] I would go to the beach and cover myself in the sand. People from different cultures and centuries have the same idea of what mermaids are ... so that's maybe a cool thing to think about.

EMMA ROBERTS

Ancient Assyria

The earliest mermaid myth so far discovered comes from Assyria, a region of Mesopotamia that would now cover parts of Iran, Iraq, Syria and Turkey. These are hot, dry parts of the world, so it's easy to see why water would be sacred. Around 1000 BC, legend tells us that the goddess Atargatis loved a human shepherd, but that she accidentally killed him – a common problem for mortals who got involved with the gods – and flung herself into a lake to hide her shame.

Atargatis the Mermaid

Initially, Atargatis became a fish but, according to legend, the waters simply couldn't hide her beauty, so she took the form of a mermaid, appearing human above the waist and as a fish below. Representations of her vary: she's sometimes seen with a human head and arms, but fish elsewhere; while on a coin from Ancient Greece, she appears as a fish with a human head.

Ancient Greece? Indeed. The appeal of Atargatis was so great that her legend spread into Greek and Roman culture, where she became the goddess Derketo to the Greeks and Dea Syria – the 'Syrian Goddess' – to the Romans.

Gorking Out

Mermaids went on to feature prominently in Greek myths and legends, with one suggesting that Thessalonike (352–295 BC), the sister of Greek commander Alexander the Great (356–323 BC), roamed the Aegean Sea as a mermaid for hundreds of years after her brother's death.

She would ask passing sailors if Alexander was alive: those who replied 'He lives and reigns and conquers the world' would pass safely; those who did not would see the mermaid become a monstrous gorgon and she would destroy their ship.

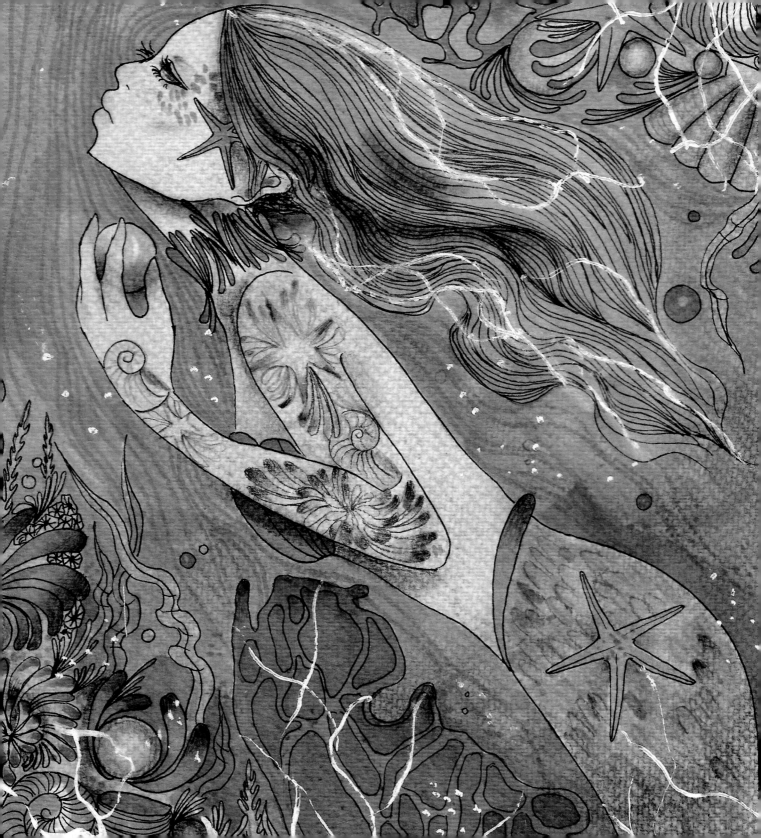

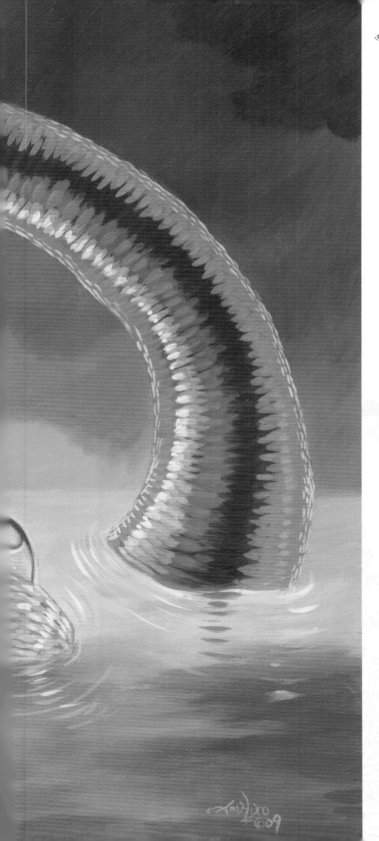

Malevolent Mermaids

Other Greek writers also mention mermaids: for Pliny (23–79 AD), mermaids were as real as fish or whales, and featured in his *Natural History* washing up on the shores of Gaul (France), their bodies covered in scales.

Seafaring women also appear in 'The Odyssey', composed by Greek poet Homer around the eighth century BC. These sirens are fearsome temptresses who try to lure the hero Odysseus and his crew on to the rocks with their bewitching singing. However, Homer's sirens are not mermaids as we know them. In fact, ancient Greek sirens were usually half-bird. Mermaids didn't inherit the dark hypnotic magic of the sirens until much later, but when they did, it was bad news for sailors, as we'll find out in the next few chapters.

Flippin' your fins, you don't get too far, legs are required for jumping, dancing!

ARIEL, DISNEY'S *THE LITTLE MERMAID*

FINS & FOLKLORE

Mermaid myths crop up in pretty much every culture and every country. They may have been inspired by the ancient Atargatis legend (see previous chapter) and spread across the world as people travelled; or they may have sprung up all by themselves. Or, of course, they might not be myths at all, but true stories of real mermaids...

Crowded Waters

There's an old Russian proverb: 'Not everything that dives into the water is a mermaid.' It's a warning to be wary of appearances, but it could also be a caution about the nature of watery creatures – they're not all benevolent, as a great number of folk tales from around the world warn.

The British Isles

If all the folk legends about mermaids around the shores of the UK are to be believed, there are so many of them that you shouldn't be able to skim a stone at the seaside without clonking some poor mermaid on the head.

The mermaids of British folklore mix the grace and wonder of Atargatis with the beguiling magic of the sirens to create luscious, lethal ladies of the waves. Here's just one example: fatally wounded by a sailor, the mermaid of Padstow, Cornwall, cursed the local waters and created the Doom Bar, a huge sandbank that has wrecked ships for centuries.

Kind Hearts and Killers

Other British mermaids are equally risky company, like the freshwater mermaid of Mermaid's Pool near Kinder Downfall in Derbyshire, who appears every year at sunrise on Easter Sunday. Peer into the pool and you might get a glimpse of your future; or the mermaid might leap out and murder you. Fun.

However, there are plenty of nice mermaids too. The ben-varrey of the Isle of Man are benevolent merpeople who use their magic to help humans, while the Irish merrows sometimes come ashore in human form and live with us for a while, perhaps even raising families, before returning to the sea.

Merfolk and Melusine

Although not technically merpeople, selkies deserve a mention – they're sea-dwelling souls, usually benevolent, who wear magical sealskins, taking them off when they want to visit dry land. The Blue Men of Muir are a touch more troublesome, and echo the legend of Thessalonike (see previous chapter). They're mermen living off the coast of northern Scotland, who enjoy creating treacherous tides and rhyming riddles for sailors. Give the wrong answer to one of their questions and they'll drag you under the waves.

Across the channel and more mysterious still is Melusine, a lady of French folklore, who made her husband promise never to spy on her in her chamber. He did, of course, and saw her in her true form – a mermaid.

Mermaids Across Europe

Mermaids live in folklore throughout Europe, some bringing us hope and happiness, and others … not so much. On the happy side, the Scandinavian Havfrue and her male counterpart, the Havman, are good-looking blue-skinned merfolk who help humans out (although fishermen believe that seeing Havfrue means a poor catch or a storm is on the way).

Elsewhere, the Polish city of Warsaw is protected by a mermaid – one legend suggests that Sawa the mermaid was rescued from captivity by Wars the fisherman. To show her gratitude, she swore to protect local fishermen, and the city's name arose from the merger of their names.

Rusalky

Further east, the Russian rusalka (plural rusalky) is a very different kind of mermaid. According to legend, they're the returned spirits of the restless dead and are always women – often those who died prematurely, through violence or drowning – who appear on riverbanks after dark.

There's some confusion about what a rusalka looks like, perhaps because of her unfortunate habit of using her dancing and singing to lure those who do see her into the water and drowning them. According to some versions of the legend, she's a classic half-woman-half-fish mermaid, but others – notably those from Siberia – suggest she's a hairy being, more like a yeti. Maybe it's a mermaid in a coat? It's really cold in Siberia.

The Inuit Mermaid

An equally cold mermaid myth comes to us from the Inuit peoples of Greenland and Canada.

Sedna is the goddess of the sea in Inuit mythology and there are many variations of the story of her birth. One in particular might appeal to mermaid lovers, describing Sedna as a beautiful maiden who rejects the attentions of all the hunters of her village. Annoyed, her father gives her to a strange, new hunter and drugs her so she can be taken away. However, when she awakes, Sedna discovers that her new husband is actually a bird spirit, and she's surrounded by birds.

There are people all over the world who carry the mermaid inside them, that otherworldly beauty and longing and desire that made her reach for heaven when she lived in the darkness of the sea.

CAROLYN TURGEON, *MERMAID*

Mother of Oceans

Her father attempts to rescue her, but the bird spirit calls up a storm. In an attempt to save her, Sedna's father casts her into the sea, where her fingers freeze off (and become all the animals of the ocean), while Sedna herself grows a fish tail and lives beneath the waves.

Perhaps unsurprisingly, this kind of treatment makes Sedna a pretty vengeful mermaid and hunters must go out of their way to appease her. If they want their hunt to be a success, they must pray to the goddess of the sea to grant them good fortune and allow them to make a good catch.

Mermaids of the Americas

What's intriguing about mermaids in both North and South America (and those further north, as above) is that they featured in the folklore of indigenous people long before Europeans ever arrived. In other words, they can't have been influenced by stories of Atargatis or other tales from across the ocean. It shows us that the link between magic, women and water is a powerful one that lives deep inside the common soul of humanity; but also perhaps that mermaids have been crossing the oceans far longer than we have.

American Girl

Two examples of mermaid tales from Native American legend show us just how universal the idea of the mermaid is. According to the Maliseet and Passamaquoddy people, Lampeqinuwok are water sprites who can appear in either human form or with fish tails. But steal their magical clothes and they become powerless – much like the European selkie.

On the rock she sat, combing her long golden hair with a comb of red gold. Her limbs were white as foam and her eyes green like the emerald green of the rushing river.

JEAN LANG, A BOOK OF MYTHS

The Passamaquoddy also tell the story of the He Nwas. In defiance of their mother, two young girls constantly swam naked in the sea to enjoy the feeling of water on their skin, until one day they couldn't leave the water: they'd swum so

much that they'd turned into mermaids, with fish tails. No problem though: they used their new forms to tow their parents' canoe.

South America and Beyond

Peru's famous refugee bear, Paddington, is a European invention. Less so is the mermaid living in the pool beneath the Gocta Cataracts, one of the world's largest waterfalls. The tale goes that she met a fisherman and granted his wish for more fish, but also slipped gold into the catch as a gift. Suspicious, the fisherman's wife followed him to the pool and saw him speaking to the mermaid – who immediately grabbed him and dragged him underwater.

Across the waters in the Caribbean, Lasirèn is a powerful Haitian mermaid prophet, who spirits women away to her underwater palace. If they survive the encounter, they return to land with the gift of foresight.

Away in Asia

Crossing the waves once more, we don't find as many mermaids in Japanese and Chinese culture. Thai folklore, however, is much more mermaid-focused. Introducing Suvannamaccha, whose name means 'Golden Mermaid' or (less poetically) 'Golden Fish'. She is a mermaid princess and lover of the Hindu monkey god Hanuman – her image features on good-luck charms throughout the country.

Far-Flung Mermaids

Beware the shores of the Philippines, which are home to the sirena – beautiful maidens with long hair and, you guessed it, fish tails. Unlike the Greek sirens, which tend to be bird-like, the sirena are fully fledged mermaids, but they share the same vicious streak: they hide amongst rocks and use their enchanting singing to lure victims near, at which point they abduct them.

What happens next varies according to who is telling the tale, but it never ends well for the luckless humans, as they're either sacrificed to the gods of the waters, or simply have the life squeezed out of them.

Java Janes

On the Indonesian island of Java, we find Nyai Loro Kidul, goddess of the sea and an important figure in Javanese folklore. Over the centuries, she has evolved into a mermaid-like being, often seen as a woman, with the lower half of a fish, bathing on the beach. Like so many mermaids, she's a perilous creature if you're a young man or a fisherman – showing us once more that the mermaid as both a deadly and divine being seems to be a universal belief around the world.

Australia and Africa

A short hop away in Australia, the native aboriginal people tell of the yawkyawk, a water spirit appearing as a young woman who is a fish below the waist. She controls the rains and is usually a kindly soul, but cross her and storms are sure to follow.

We end our mermaid safari where human civilization began: in Africa, where water deities have blessed the rains and rivers for thousands of years. One group is known as Mami Wata (which literally means 'mother of water' in Pidgin English), who look very mermaid-like (with the addition of a big snake wrapped around them) and who have power over life-giving water, just like the yawkyawk. They also share qualities with Lasirèn of Haiti, after the tradition was carried from Africa to the Caribbean with the transport of slaves.

So many mermaids, so many myths, but so much in common. It's almost as if the mermaids were the same, doing their thing in the ocean, and only the people watching them were different.

MERMAIDS ON STRANGER TIDES

Historically, it hasn't been that hard to spook a sailor. The sea was a perilous highway for the wooden ships of the past, so it's not surprising that sailors harboured all manner of superstitions and beliefs that either explained bad luck, helped predict it, or drove it away. Some of those superstitions included avoiding having bananas on board (seriously) and a belief that redheads were unlucky. Sure enough, mermaids feature too, and beliefs about them abound on ships and on shore.

Making Up the Mermaid

Given the amount of time sailors spent at sea, it's hardly surprising that they had

a hand in the myth of the mermaid. There's an order of aquatic mammals called sirenia, which includes manatees and dugongs, both of which look something like a cross between a seal, a cow and a slightly sad balloon. From a distance, their heads bobbing in the water could look a bit human, and early seafarers would certainly have encountered them in many parts of the world, so add a bit of imagination (and a few shots of rum) and it's possible that manatees became mermaids in the tall tales of sailors.

Darwin may have been quite correct in his theory that man descended from the apes of the forest, but surely woman rose from the frothy sea. MARGOT DATZ, A SURVIVAL GUIDE FOR LANDLOCKED MERMAIDS

You Always Take the Weather With You

As we saw in the previous chapter, various cultures shared similar beliefs that an encounter with a mermaid meant a watery grave. Simply spotting one might be a bad omen, foretelling a long trip, rough seas or even the shadow of death on the waves.

Britain offers a couple of examples. Hear mermaids singing from Cornwall's Mermaid's Rock (the clue's in the name) and a ship will sink nearby within the week. Likewise, some versions of the folk ballad 'Sir Patrick Spens' feature a mermaid warning the crew of a sailing vessel that their voyage is doomed.

Mixed Fortunes

Not all beliefs around mermaids are born of fear though. For the sailors of Trinidad and Tobago,

merpeople are benevolent spirits who can bring luck, fortune and even intelligence and imagination (they'd be handy to have around at exam time).

Other superstitions acknowledge that mermaids' gifts can be a double-edged sword. Take Lutey Cury, a fisherman from another Cornish myth (are there any actual people in Cornwall, or just merfolk and legends?), who is granted three wishes by a mermaid but must then join her in the sea after nine years. As must one of his descendants, every nine years after that...

Who would be
A mermaid fair,
Singing alone,
Combing her hair
Under the sea,
In a golden curl
With a comb of pearl,
On a throne?

ALFRED, LORD TENNYSON, *THE MERMAID*

Never Cross a Mermaid

Sailors knew to respect mermaids and certainly never to do one harm. Hurt one, wrong one, maybe look at one funny, and you'll invite chaos on your crew. In some versions, the mermaid's curse might doom your ship to wander for ever and never reach land; in others, the seas will rise and strike you down. One Irish legend, for example, tells of a sailor who killed a mermaid and who was subsequently chased by vengeful waves every time he went to sea, until he was eventually drowned.

Beauty seems to be the keynote of the water spirits. Wherever we find them pictured in art or sculpture, they abound in symmetry and grace.

MANLY P. HALL,
THE SECRET TEACHINGS OF ALL AGES

Making Peace With the Merpeople

Knowing about their touchy tempers, some sailors try to make peace with mermaids. Mami Wata are fond of shiny trinkets and pampering – aren't we all? – so offerings to them include jewellery, perfume and other knick-knacks. The Inuit, meanwhile, make offerings to Sedna in the hope of a fruitful sea hunt; in one version of the myth a shaman even offers to comb and braid her hair.

Wooden Women

While it's now been chucked into the bin marked 'stupid', for a long time, sailors held the belief that having a woman on board was unlucky. In a classic example of having your cake and eating it, the solution was to put, um, naked women – often mermaids – on the prow of the ship, in the form of a carved wooden figure. The sailors were adamant – they would be – that only a naked woman would calm the sea gods and give the ship safe passage.

Intriguingly, a potential side effect of this superstition could have been to carry the European image of the mermaid to indigenous cultures, like the Inuit or Native Americans, influencing the way mermaids were (and are) described in their folk tales.

Ariel, listen to me. The human world is a mess. Life under the sea is better than anything they got up there.

SEBASTIAN, DISNEY'S *THE LITTLE MERMAID*

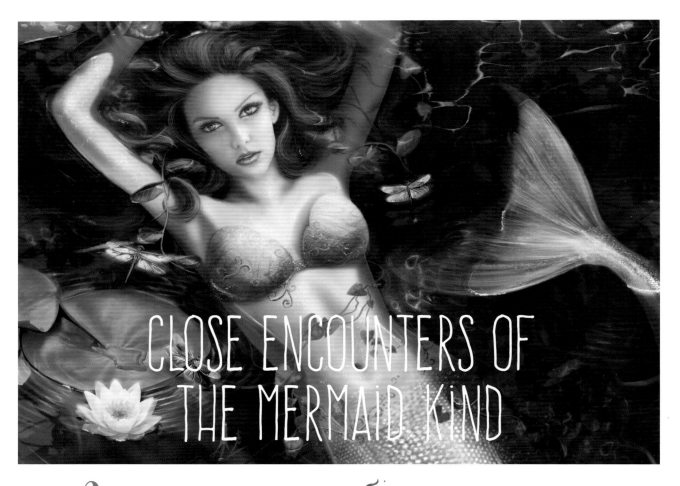

CLOSE ENCOUNTERS OF THE MERMAID KIND

Myths, superstitions and folk fables are all well and good, but it's possible that mermaids wouldn't hold such fascination for us if there weren't another kind of story out there as well: tales of mermaid sightings. Through the ages there have been reports of encounters with merfolk all over the world. Are they all hoaxes?

Cases of mistaken identity? Or, in amongst all the tall tales, are there some true stories of real-life rendezvous?

Columbus and the Mermaids

Italian explorer Christopher Columbus (1451–1506) is credited with many achievements, including charting some of the earliest sailing routes to

the Americas from Europe (and, less gloriously, establishing the transatlantic slave trade).

During his first voyage, he wrote that he had spotted three mermaids at play in the Caribbean surf in early January 1493. His record sounds a little disappointed, as he remarked that they were 'not half as beautiful as they are painted'. It's more likely that he saw manatees and was confused – after all, he had been at sea on and off since August the previous year.

Many Manatees

The big, gentle manatee is probably behind many historical mermaid sightings. English sailor and explorer John Smith (1580–1631) is perhaps better known for his part in the story of Pocahontas, but during his exploration of what is now the US, particularly Massachusetts, he claimed to have seen a mermaid off the coast.

According to Smith, the mermaid was 'by no means unattractive' and had long green hair. However, as manatees are known to still occasionally appear in the waters of the region, there's a good chance that they were the beings he saw. It's anyone's guess how a capable explorer like Smith would mistake a blubbery manatee for a ravishing mermaid. Rum, anyone?

The fairest of maidens is sitting
Unwittingly wondrous up there,
Her golden jewels are shining,
She's combing her golden hair.

HEINRICH HEINE, *LORELEI*
(TRANSLATION BY A.Z. FOREMAN)

The comb she holds is golden,
She sings a song as well
Whose melody binds an enthralling
And overpowering spell.

HEINRICH HEINE, *LORELEI*
(TRANSLATION BY A.Z. FOREMAN)

Yo Ho Ho

Speaking of rum, even hardened pirates like Blackbeard (real name Edward Teach, 1680–1718) claimed to have seen mermaids on their travels. The legendary pirate is said to have spotted mermaids and gave orders to avoid certain locations as a result. Pirates, perhaps even more than regular sailors, were a superstitious bunch: they believed mermaids would bewitch them into giving up their ill-gotten gold before sending them to the bottom of the sea.

Other sailors of the seventeenth century had merfolk encounters, including the crew of the Danish ship *Oldenborg*. They sighted a merman off the coast of Africa in 1672; the ship's doctor drew a sketch of what he saw, and it is now in the Royal Danish Library.

Scottish Sightings

If you really want to see a mermaid in the wild though, best wrap up warm, as the northern coast of Scotland and its islands have hosted many alleged mermaid meet-ups over the years. They include an encounter on Benbecula, in the Outer Hebrides, in 1830, where locals spotted

and subsequently killed a strange being on the beach. Contemporary descriptions say the creature had the body of a child but with abnormally large breasts, and that its lower half was like a salmon without scales. It was apparently buried close by, but no grave has ever been found.

Sea Monkeys

Other nineteenth-century Scottish sightings include a crofter on Barra spotting an otter, which (when viewed through a telescope) turned out to be a bare-breasted woman holding a child, who then dived beneath the waves.

Then there was Dr Robert Hamilton, a professor at the University of Edinburgh, who reported that a mermaid had been captured by some Shetland fisherman, but released when it began moaning. Hamilton's mermaid had a monkey's face, a woman's torso and a dogfish's tail, which gives it a similar appearance to the mermaid at the centre of American showman P.T. Barnum's 'Feejee Mermaid' hoax of 1842.

Faking It

Barnum's fake (bought from a sailor) – actually the head and torso of a monkey stitched to the tail of a fish – was passed off as a mermaid and displayed in a New York museum, attracting a curious public. Although the original 'disappeared', it was copied many times over in lurid nineteenth-century sideshows.

Hoax or not, modern-day sightings of mermaids continue. In 2009, many people reported a mermaid frolicking in the waters of Haifa Bay near the Israeli town of Kiryat Yam; in Zimbabwe, no

Her hair was as a wet fleece of gold, and each separate hair as a thread of line gold in a cup of glass. Her body was as white ivory, and her tail was of silver and pearl. Silver and pearl was her tail, and the green weeds of the sea coiled round it; and like sea-shells were her ears, and her lips were like sea-coral. The cold waves dashed over her cold breasts, and the salt glistened upon her eyelids.

OSCAR WILDE, *THE FISHERMAN AND HIS SOUL*

less a person than the water resources minister reported that work on two reservoirs had to be halted because mermaids were hounding the work crews. Hoaxes? Real meetings? Reservoir dogs? We'll never know, but it shows that the allure of the mermaid – if nothing else – is definitely alive and well in the twenty-first century.

TALL TAILS: MERMAIDS IN STORIES & POETRY

Mermaids have swum through the pages of some of the most popular stories ever told. They're a gift for poets, authors and comic artists, as they're familiar characters to all of us in one way: we all think we know what a mermaid looks like, and how they behave. But do we? That's where the fun starts. Writers have frequently played with the idea of the mermaid, making them do unexpected things or changing the way they look.

The Little Mermaid

Starting with the traditional, Hans Christian Andersen's (1805–75) fairytale, *The Little*

Mermaid (1837), is probably responsible for shaping the way many of us in modern culture think of mermaids: beautiful, romantic beings with love for people in their hearts.

The fairytale is a little – OK, a lot – darker than the Disney movie. Andersen's mermaid falls in love with a prince and in order to try to win his heart, agrees to take a potion that will give her legs but remove her voice, doom her soul and make her feel like she's walking on knives. For ever.

It was wonderful the songs they'd sing – like the sound of the sea set to music was what my mother told me, and she was told by them that knew.

GEORGE A. BIRMINGHAM, *THE MERMAID*

Out of the Sea

She agrees to this trade, but fails to win the heart of the prince – the only thing that could save her from turning into sea foam – and so throws herself into the sea to die. Not many singing crabs here.

The mermaid's soul is eventually saved though, and she's reborn as a spirit of the air. What's the moral? There are many possibilities: that it's better to be yourself and stick to what you know; that a good heart will be rewarded in eternity; or, more pessimistically, simply that love sucks. And hurts. That's the beauty of the mermaid – she's mysterious. It's up to each of us to work out what she means.

Time and Tides

Mermaids in fiction occur way before Andersen's tale though, and have continued right up to the present day. The fantastical *One Thousand*

and One Nights, sometimes called The Arabian Nights, is a collection of Middle Eastern folk tales collected between the eighth and thirteenth centuries, in which Princess Scheherazade spins yarns for her prince, many of them containing encounters with merfolk. One, 'The Adventures of Bulukiya', features an entire mermaid world.

The little sea maid sang the most sweetly of all, and the whole court applauded her, and for a moment she felt gay in her heart, for she knew that she had the loveliest voice of all in the sea or on the earth.

HANS CHRISTIAN ANDERSEN, THE LITTLE MERMAID

Other classic encounters include cameos in Shakespeare's A Midsummer Night's Dream (c. 1595) and Oscar Wilde's The Fisherman and His Soul (1891). More modern encounters include a distant glimpse of mermaids in 'The

Voyage of the Dawn Treader' (1952), part of C.S. Lewis's *The Chronicles of Narnia*, or the *Fins* series (2010–12) from Tera Lynn Childs, which features a mermaid princess.

Darker Waters

They also appear in *Harry Potter and the Goblet of Fire* (J.K. Rowling, 2000), where their songs are painful shrieks above the water but melodious chants beneath it. In both book and film, they are wild, tribal beings, far removed from the stunning sirens of Andersen's fairytale, decked out in bead necklaces and menacing Harry with tridents.

I would comb my hair
till my ringlets would fall,
Low adown, low adown,
From under my starry
sea-bud crown

ALFRED, LORD TENNYSON,
THE MERMAID

Some mermaids don't even need to be seen to create an air of dread. Reading *Moby Dick* (Herman Melville, 1851) is as close as any of us are likely to get to sailing on a whaling ship. The strange cries in the dark were taken by the sailors to be mermaids cursing them. Their grim captain, Ahab, laughs it off, but a crew member dies the next day, to the sailors' terror.

Other Incarnations

You'll find mermaids splashing around in all manner of other stories. *The Moon and the Sun* (Vonda N. McIntyre, 1997) sees a mermaid captured by scientists and brought to the French court of Louis XIV. Meanwhile, Superman's first girlfriend in the 1950s comics was, believe it or not, the mermaid Lori Lemaris.

She is one of many comic-book mermaids of course. Other examples include the girl group of mermaids who feature in the extraordinarily named *Mermaid Melody Pichi Pichi Pitch* (2002–05), a Japanese manga series (also an anime series), and use their singing voices as a weapon.

She Sells Sea Shells

As sometimes-romantic beings lounging on seashores, mermaids were inevitably going to attract the attention of a poet or two, like Alfred, Lord Tennyson (1809–92), whose 'The Mermaid' (1830) imagines love as a kind of death and paints the mermaid herself as a sometimes vain, sometimes lonely being, brushing her hair and brushing away lovers.

Mermaids close out the poem 'Prufrock' (1915) by T.S. Eliot (1888–1965) with the lines 'I hear the mermaids singing / I do not think they will sing to me'. These are not literal mermaids, but imagined ones, symbolizing something beautiful but just out of reach of the poet as he struggles with his place in the world. Just like a mermaid to inspire and frustrate at the same time.

FINSTAGRAM: MERMAIDS IN ART

Mermaids have inspired artists to create sculptures, carvings, woodcuts, paintings, book illustrations and much more, and they continue to do so today. Over the centuries, the image of the mermaid has shifted around until it settled on the form we all recognize, and when we explore the world of art, we're likely to encounter as many different kinds of mermaid as there are beneath the waves.

Sacred Mermaids

Among the earliest images of mermaids that still survive are those carved on to the walls of

churches, and that tells us something about just how important mermaids have been to society throughout the ages. Building a church at any time was expensive, difficult and time-consuming, and nothing appears on a church accidentally.

Mermaids on churches like the Norman Chapel in Durham Castle, England (1078) or the Rio Mau Monastic Church, Portugal (1151) carried a message to the faithful: to beware the sins of the flesh that these temptresses symbolized. It's also quite possible that they appealed to lusty stonemasons and daydreaming churchgoers.

Two by Two

These mermaids were preceded by images on Greek and Roman tombs and still more sacred mermaids came after them. There are examples of religious art featuring mermaids from all over the world, from a wooden chair in Cornwall from the sixteenth century to a fountain in Mexico City from the seventeenth.

Perhaps even more curious is a woodcut illustration that accompanied a German edition of the Bible produced in 1483 by Anton Koberger (c.1440–1513). Alongside the story of the flood and Noah's Ark is an image showing the Ark and, bobbing in the water alongside it, a mer-family (and a creature that's either a seal or their mer-dog).

Fine Art Mermaids

Mermaids have been such potent muses for artists that it's impossible to cram all the examples into these pages, so we'll have to make do with dipping our toes into the water.

We'll start in Marseilles, where Marie de'Medici, new queen of France, is being welcomed into her new country. Not that you'd notice, because the foreground of Peter Paul Rubens' painting The *Arrival of Marie de' Medici at Marseilles* (c. 1622–25) is taken up with voluptuous sea nymphs who totally upstage her.

Rubens' mermaids are vigorous and powerful, but later visions offer different takes on the mermaid. Frederic Leighton's *The Fisherman and the Syren* (1856) has a helpless man swooning in the arms of a mermaid on the shore, showing her seductive lure.

She had sad green eyes
and long green hair.
When he looked closer he
saw that she had a long
bright tail instead of legs,
but he thought her very
beautiful all the same.

MARY DE MORGAN, *THROUGH THE FIRE*

Shadows on the Waves

Edvard Munch, meanwhile, offers a stern and forbidding figure frowning from murky water in *The Lady from the Sea* (1896), while Gustav Klimt's *Mermaids* (1899) peer glumly from shrouded bodies in pea-soup seas.

These are mermaids from the dark corners of our subconscious, not beautiful nymphs on a bright shore.

Peter … would come up with mermaid scales still sticking to him, and yet not be able to say for certain what had been happening. It was really rather irritating to children who had never seen a mermaid.

J.M. BARRIE, *PETER PAN*

Other artists took liberties with mythology to create their own interpretations. *Ulysses and the Sirens* by Herbert James Draper (1909) shows the Sirens, who are usually bird-like, as mermaids – all beautiful, some with fish tails, all lunging at Ulysses. It's a painting that fits in with the repressed English society of the time, where sex and female beauty were taboo and looking at naked ladies in paintings was safer and more appropriate.

The Classic Mermaid

There's no single painting responsible for creating the twenty-first-century ideal of the mermaid, but *The Mermaid* by John William

Waterhouse (1901) was (and remains) particularly influential. His mermaid sits combing her long red hair on the beach, silvery tail gleaming as the sea breaks around her; she is clear-eyed, polished and perfect.

Not that men are the only ones to have painted mermaids. Elisabeth Jerichau Baumann's *Havfrue* (1873) is particularly intriguing. Her mermaid gazes out at us from the shallows and is much more clearly a sea-being than Waterhouse's mermaid: she comes draped in seaweed and her hair is matted with kelp, yet she remains beautiful. Her expression seems to change, depending on your mood.

The Little Mermaid

We can't end anywhere but in Copenhagen, birthplace of Hans Christian Andersen, where the most famous mermaid of them all has sat since 1913. Edvard Eriksen's bronze statue of Andersen's mermaid is modelled partly on ballet dancer Ellen Price (who played the mermaid in the ballet version of the tale) and partly on his wife. She is visited by over one million tourists every year, as she reclines on her rock at the water's edge and looks on while mermaid parades go past in her honour.

SONGS OF THE SIRENS

Appropriately for romantic beings who spend a lot of their time singing, mermaids have inspired their fair share of fin-folk anthems over the centuries.

They vary from tragic nineteenth-century love poems set to music, to boisterous sea shanties, to glossy contemporary pop songs. These musical mermaids are a mixed crowd: some are lovelorn souls drowning in their broken hearts; others are malign beings intent on drowning someone else; and others are just an excuse for pop stars to dress up as mermaids – but who can blame them for that?

Sea Songs

Mermaids are regular characters in traditional folk music, with its story-based songs that often combine myth, magic and folklore. A particularly

spirited number is 'The Mermaid Song', which dates to some time in the eighteenth century and tells the tale of a ship heading out to sea and encountering a mermaid combing her hair, who gives the crew a cheerful prediction:

'Then up spoke the captain of our gallant ship,
And a brave old man was he,

He said, "This fishy mermaid
has warned me of our doom:

We shall sink to the bottom of the sea!"'

Various crew members – including a smug parrot – then explain why they're not keen on that idea, before the ship inevitably sinks and all hands are lost. Except for the parrot.

Folk and Fins

Other mermaid-themed folk tunes include 'The Keeper of the Eddystone Light', another eighteenth-century shanty telling of the singer's parents: a mermaid and a human lighthouse keeper. More contemporary folk musicians include Joanna Newsom, whose 2007 song 'Colleen' features a woman haunted by dreams of a past life in the sea – it's never clear whether she's truly a mermaid or not.

I think that the waves will devour
The boatman and boat as one;
And this by her song's sheer power
Fair Lorelei has done.

HEINRICH HEINE, *LORELEI*
(TRANSLATION BY A.Z. FOREMAN)

Lamenting Lorelei

Also ambiguous are the Lorelei, famous sirens from German folklore. Strictly speaking, they are more haunting water spirit than mermaid. But as muses go, Lorelei are up there with the best mermaids: a poem about one by Heinrich Heine in 1824 was later set to music by classical composers Friedrich Silcher (1837) and Franz Liszt (1841).

Mermaids, and water spirits in general, do seem to make beautiful classical music happen. Melusine (*see* page 31) is immortalized in 'Fair Melusina' by Felix Mendelssohn (1834), while those German river ladies crop up again in Richard Wagner's *Ring of the Nibelung*, an epic musical drama steeped in Norse mythology and written over more than two decades (1848–74).

Pop Goes the Mermaid

Lorelei crop up in pop too. In 1998, Eagle Eye Cherry's 'When Mermaids Cry' reimagined the siren as a mermaid, while other pop musicians have also embraced their inner mermaid: Madonna featured them in the songs 'Cherish' (1988) and 'Music' (2000); Ke$ha went full psychedelia as a mermaid in the video to 'Your Love is my Drug' (2010); Lady Gaga's 'You and I' video (2010) cast her as mermaid, gills and all; and Katy Perry showed up as a mermaid during her 2011 'California Dreams' tour.

Play On

Pop, folk, classical – there's room for musical mermaids of all kinds and they continue to inspire. In late 2017, the Northern Ballet company unveiled a new production of 'The Little Mermaid', based on the fairytale and with all new music – so the song of the mermaids is still in our heads, even now.

MAKING A SPLASH: MERMAIDS IN FILM & TV

Magic, mystery, the lure of the sea and sometimes a pretty face? It's no wonder the cameras came calling for mermaids. The very first mermaid on film appeared in 1904 in a short silent feature by George Méliès, simply called *The Mermaid.*

A few years later, Annette Kellerman (1887–1975) was the first actor to swim in a mermaid costume on film in *Siren of the Sea* (1911). A champion swimmer, Kellerman made an extraordinary mermaid, doing her own stunts (including diving 60 feet into a pool of crocodiles) and pioneering one-piece swimwear for women.

Swimming Sixties

It may seem hard to believe now, but before Kellerman, women generally wore a combination of dresses and pantaloons (like trousers) to swim. Kellerman's fame enabled her to launch her own line of rather more practical swimwear – even though wearing it on a beach in 1907 got her arrested for indecency – and become an advocate for health and fitness. Just one way that mermaids have helped make the world a little better for women.

Times moved on for screen mermaids as well as swimwear, of course, and by the 1960s, they were appearing as puppets (albeit with legs) in TV show *Stingray* (1964) and brat-pack rom com *Beach Blanket Bingo* (1965).

Splashing Around

Bigger roles were to follow a few decades later as the 1980s brought mermaids back to the big screen. Whimsical, slow-burning and faintly magical, *Local Hero* (1984) is mainly about the collision of the oil business with a sleepy Scottish town, but in a quirky subplot, it's hinted that the marine researcher Marina (played by Jenny Seagrove) is actually a mermaid.

Come from the sea,
Maiden, to me,
Maiden of mystery, love, and pain!
Wake from thy sleep,
Low in the deep,
Over thy green waves sport again!

JAMES HOGG, *THE MAID OF THE SEA*

There's no doubt about the mermaid status of Darryl Hannah's character Madison in *Splash* (1984) though – she can leave the sea to walk around and fall in love with Tom Hanks, the king of 1980s comedy, but if she gets wet, her tail will reappear. The story is a loose riff on *The Little Mermaid*, of course, but with rather more slapstick and a happier ending.

They were faire ladies,
till they fondly striv'd
With th'Heliconian maides
for maystery;
Of whom they, over-comen,
were depriv'd
Of their proud beautie,
and th'one moyity
Transform'd to fish for their
bold surquedry;
But th'upper half their
hew retayned still,
And their sweet skill in
wonted melody;
Which ever after they
abused to ill,
T'allure weake travellers,
whom gotten they did kill

EDMUND SPENSER, *THE FAERIE QUEEN*

Disney Does Mermaids

And speaking of that little mermaid, in 1989, Disney changed the game entirely with their animated take on the Hans Christian Andersen fairytale. A few things set the movie apart: first, there's the mermaid herself, the winsome Ariel, an independent soul determined to make her own destiny rather than have it happen to her; then there's the totally rewritten plot, the happy ending, and the throwing out of all that glum 'dying as sea foam' business.

*Many tales
I've been told
of sailors
having died.
After seeing
a mermaid
known
Known as Lorelei*

EAGLE EYE CHERRY, WHEN MERMAIDS CRY

There's also the music. The centrepiece of the film is the rousing 'Under the Sea', which went on to win an Oscar, Golden Globe and Grammy – not bad for a tune belted out by a singing crab with a backing band of molluscs.

Part of Our World

The Little Mermaid reimagined the mermaid as a pop-culture princess, making her a relatable teenager wanting to grow up and yet cling to her trinkets at the same time. While the movie was criticized by some (as many Disney movies are) for leaning too heavily on the whole 'romantic love is all that matters' thing, others saw the birth of an aquatic icon. Ariel has certainly been lodged in our heads and hearts ever since.

She did more than make us all hum 'Part of Your World' though. The success of *The Little Mermaid* was a shot in the arm for Disney and the wider animation world. Its global success led to the company making more animated films and developing new technology, all of which led to *Beauty and the Beast* (1991), *Aladdin* (1992) and *The Lion King* (1994) – and from there to Pixar, Dreamworks and the birth of movies like the *Toy Story* series (1995–2010), *Wall-E* (2008) and the peerless *Up* (2009) and *Inside Out* (2015).

A mermaid
found a
swimming lad,
Picked him up
for her own,
Pressed her body
to his body,
Laughed; and plunging down
Forgot in cruel happiness
That even lovers drown.

W.B. YEATS, *THE MERMAID*

Lost Boys and Barbie Dolls

Meanwhile, other mermaids were doing brisk business in other movies. They've bothered Peter Pan to varying degrees over the years in story and film, and crop up in *Peter Pan* (1953) as well as *Hook* (1991) and *Peter Pan* reprised in 2003; in the last, they're a little less cheery than Ariel, attempting to drown Wendy.

Showing just how diverse their appearances are, mermaids also feature in a range of Barbie movies, as well as playing against Captain Jack Sparrow in *Pirates of the Caribbean: On Stranger Tides* (2011). They're slightly different in each onscreen incarnation – some are daft and magical, some surly but helpful, some downright dangerous – showing once again how unpredictable mermaid kind can be, a little like the sea itself.

Taking Over TV

The small screen has also had plenty of fun with mermaids. One of the earliest Japanese anime to

be dubbed and screened in the US and UK was *Marine Boy* (1967 onwards), about a martial-arts expert with a high-tech wetsuit who nonetheless spent a lot of time getting knocked out and needing his mermaid pal, Neptina, to rescue him.

Mermaids also featured in the weird, dark *Mermaid Saga* anime (1984–94), in which eating a mermaid either makes you live for ever, die horribly or turn into a wretched mutant (yikes). They've also appeared in *Power Rangers*, *Family Guy* and even an episode of *Dr Who* ('The Curse of the Black Spot', 2011).

The Great Fake

Different again is hit Australian show *H2O: Just Add Water*, which imagines the lives of three teenage girls who become mermaids after an accident with some moonlight, a dormant volcano and a mysterious cave (it was one of those parties). The girls can live normal lives but become mermaids within seconds of getting wet; this isn't always bad, and on the upside they also gain magical power over water. The show's blend of *Buffy the Vampire Slayer*-esque magic-as-burden themes and *Splash* goofiness have earned it a worldwide audience of 250 million.

But at night I would wander away, away,
I would fling on each side my low-flowing locks,
And lightly vault from the throne and play
With the mermen in and out of the rocks
ALFRED, LORD TENNYSON, *THE MERMAID*

Finally, a special mention for the folks at Animal Planet, who created mermaid mockumentaries *Mermaids: The Body Found* (2012) and *Mermaids: The New Evidence* (2013). These treat mermaids as real subjects and feature video 'evidence', interviews and scientific theories. After the shows aired, the US National Ocean Service had to release a statement explaining that 'no evidence of aquatic humanoids has ever been found' in response to enquiries from the public. But maybe they just wanted to keep the mermaids for themselves.

I would be a mermaid fair;
I would sing to myself the
whole of the day;
With a comb of pearl I
would comb my hair;
And still as I comb'd I
would sing and say,
"Who is it loves me? Who
loves not me?"

ALFRED, LORD TENNYSON, *THE MERMAID*

MODERN MERMAIDS

Where can you see mermaids today? You could always take the traditional route and lurk on the seashore, or perhaps become a superstitious sailor with a habit of attracting bad luck, but there are easier options. In fact, mermaids are never far from our sides, if you know where to look. Only they're no longer carved into churches or hiding in sea shanties: they're in every kind of media, every style of art and even every smartphone now that mermaid emoji have been born.

Professional Mermaids

A fine example of just how important mermaids remain to us is the existence

of the professional mermaid (and merman). These aren't just bored souls in seashell bras: mermaid Grace, a professional mermaid in the UK, is a model but also a qualified free diver, specially trained to hold her breath for minutes at a time while performing in her mermaid costume, either at parties, displays or fashion shoots.

There are mermaids like Grace all over the world, and they meet at the 'Miss Mermaid International' contest every year. Contenders have to show off various mermaid qualities, including swimming in their mermaid tails and striking a pose by the sea.

One Friday morn when
we set sail
And out ship not far
from land,
We there did espy a fair
pretty maid,
With a comb and a glass
in her hand.

THE MERMAID, TRADITIONAL FOLK SONG

Dive! Dive! Dive!

In case you've never encountered it before, free diving is pretty much what it sounds like: deep diving, but free of breathing apparatus. It takes

skill, practice and a lot of training to do safely, so please don't strap on some fins and leg it down the quarry, OK?

Take the Japanese Ama, who have been skin diving – a kind of traditional free diving – for more than two thousand years. Mainly women, they dive for shellfish and are often thought of as mermaids.

Even more mermaid-like are the female diving pros at Florida's Weeki Wachee Springs, where 'live mermaids' (actually certified divers) have performed underwater shows for the public since 1947. All the mermaids have special costumed tails and entertain the crowds while holding their breath.

The dolphin wheels,
the sea-cows snort,
And unseen mermaids'
pearly song
Comes bubbling up,
the weeds among.

THOMAS LOVELL BEDDOES,
SAILOR'S SONG

113

one particularly famous mermaid pretty regularly, looking out at you from the cups and counters of your friendly neighbourhood Starbucks coffee shop.

The Starbucks mermaid is an unusual one, more akin to the snake-like image of Melusine in some versions of the myth (*see* page 31), as she actually has a split tail. The very first Starbucks logo was brown and looked more like a woodcut, and clearly showed a split-tailed mermaid with bare breasts.

Icons

Over time, the Starbucks design has been refined into something more stylized and also a bit more chaste: the latest version is zoomed right in so you only see a hint of twin tail and, these days, the mermaid's flowing locks are covering her breasts. She's a sleek, modern spin on a classic look.

And speaking of sleek looks, the mermaid in modern culture pops up in more places than just coffee cups. Mermaid Barbie is now offering a new generation the chance to play at sea siren (oddly enough, there's not much on the box about curses and drowning and suchlike).

Hiding in Plain Sight

You don't actually need to head to Florida (although apparently it's nice there) to see mermaids. There's a good chance you see

Updating the Mermaid Look

Many modern mermaids are a long way from the curvy paintings of the Victorian era, the sinister, sinful creatures of mythology, or the bloodthirsty sirens of folk tales and sea shanties. They're much cleaner and calmer, and tend to show up wearing a lot more glitter – although Disney's Ariel does crop up in all manner of internet memes – often heavily tattooed(!)

The twenty-first-century mermaid is a much more benign being. They're like their kindred magical beings, unicorns: once fearsome and deadly, now they offer playful escapism, fun and froth. After centuries of ambiguous mayhem, that might not be such a bad thing. And when Kim Kardashian is dressing as a mermaid, you know for sure they've arrived.

Out of the Sea

If you want to get involved with mermaid culture, there are so many options. They're a popular tattoo choice, for example, but for something rather less permanent, you'll find infinite t-shirts with mermaid slogans on. Or you could go one further and get into a little mermaid cosplay: tails are easier to come by than ever before, and you don't need to fling yourself into the sea, get bewitched or anything – just browse the internet. YouTube is crammed with mermaid makeup tutorials that will give you that seaside shimmer. There's so much to explore – and it's all proof that the appeal of the mermaid is undimmed. Even though they're not trying to wreck our ships any more, the sea maidens are still singing their alluring song to us.

A MERMAID SPEAKS!

Mermaid Grace is a **professional mermaid based in the UK,** although she works in water all over the world. Here's what life as a mermaid is like, in her own words...

Why do mermaids appeal to you?

Mermaids appeal to me for several reasons – the long beautiful hair, the magic, the wonder – but mostly for me it's their amazing singing voices and that they live in the ocean. My biggest passion in life is singing and I have always been infatuated with the ocean; no matter how down or unwell I'm feeling, if I can just get into a body of water, I immediately feel better.

Why did you want to be a professional mermaid?

I love to perform and I'm a bit of a Disney fanatic, so I started working as a princess for children's parties and events. My favourite princess was of course Ariel, but I could never portray her as realistically as I wanted to. I thought, wouldn't it be fantastic if I could be a real mermaid swimming around? I had always wanted to be one and if I can be a convincing princess, perhaps being a mermaid is a possibility? After a lot of research, training and preparation, I became a professional mermaid and I absolutely love what I do.

She sinks into her spell:
and when full soon
Her lips move and she soars
into her song,
What creatures of the
midmost main shall throng

DANTE GABRIEL ROSSETTI, A SEA SPELL

What kind of reaction do you get from people?

People react in all sorts of ways: children can occasionally be scared at first; they've never seen a real mermaid before! But most young ones and adults alike are in absolute awe when they see me perform. I'm a qualified free diver so being underwater for so long seems amazing to spectators.

Got any advice for anyone wanting to follow in your fin-steps?

My biggest piece of advice for anyone wanting to be a professional mermaid is to do your research first, and don't expect it to be easy – especially when living in colder countries. Many pools won't allow you to use your fin to swim, so keeping up with your training is difficult. It also takes a long time to build up a reputation as a professional mermaid. I always tell anyone considering this as a career path, or even as a serious hobby, to get some free-diving training first. Mermaiding is perfectly safe, but only when done correctly – getting qualified as a free diver taught me everything I needed to know about holding my breath and diving deep waters without putting myself in danger. It also gives clients the peace of mind that you know what you're doing.

What's the best thing about being a mermaid?

It's hard to pinpoint just one thing. It's great fun explaining what I do to others, they're always so interested; and I love being in the water. But I guess the best thing has to be using the magical fantasy of mermaids to get children interested in marine conservation. *You can find out more about Grace and her work at hireamermaid.co.uk.*

A POSITIVE FORCE

The history of mermaids is certainly a magical one. They began as ancient water goddesses, found their form through myth, fable and more than the occasional yarn from a drunken sailor, and gradually evolved from life-giving sacred spirit to fearful sea being, to today's graceful, positive souls.

A Universal Being

Mermaids have arrived in the modern world after a long journey through art, myth, religion and even the movies, to become so famous that you could ask almost anyone to describe a mermaid and they'd tell you more or less the same thing. That's pretty impressive. So what lessons can they offer us after all that time?

Mermaids For Ever

Maybe most importantly of all, mermaids can carry a message to every society, everywhere, that women are strong, powerful and – like the sea – are creators of life, the most magical thing of all. They both – women, and the seas on which we depend – deserve respect. Mermaids can also stand for independence, daring, romance, beauty; all the good stuff, really. Their example can inspire us to love without fear, to explore, be playful, be compassionate to one another, to embrace things and people who are a little different, and also not to take any nonsense. You don't want to mess with an angry mermaid, after all.

Finally, they act as a constant reminder that in life, it's always good to look beyond the surface of things and explore the depths. After all, that's where the mermaids are.

> *Come down to the sea,*
> *give yourself up to me*
> *Come down to the sea,*
> *give yourself up to me*

THE BEARD AND THE MERMAID, *THE FILEY MERMAID*

RESOURCES

Some extra bits of finned fun and frolics.

Mermaids on the Page

The Mermaid and Mrs Hancock,
Imogen Hermes Gowar (2018)
Historical literary fiction set in eighteenth-century London. Has Captain Hancock truly found a mermaid at sea? And what will it mean for his life, and the lives of those around him? A heady brew of mystery, desire, warm wit and unlikely romance awaits...

The Mermaid Trials, Cameron Drake (2018)
A cross between *The Hunger Games* and *The Little Mermaid*, this series follows the fate of merpeople forced to battle one another for the amusement of the Royals.

Mermaids: An Anthology, Steve Dobell (2013)
A compilation of mermaid-themed fine art paired with excerpts from folk tales, poems and songs, ideal for inspiring romantic mermaid daydreams.

The Singing Mermaid, Julia Donaldson and Lydia Monks (2013)
A rhyming children's picture book by one of the biggest names in the game (Julia D created the Gruffalo), all about the plight of a mermaid lured away to the circus but desperate to return to the sea. Adventurous, fun and also – literally – full of glitter.

The Secret History of Mermaids, Ari Berk (2009)
Entirely bonkers romp through merfolk myth and legend, as seen through the fictional Order of the Golden Quill, featuring some facts, some fancy, and lots of lovely (and slightly mad) illustrations.

Mermaids: The Myths, Legends, and Lore, Skye Alexander (2012)
Lots of detail on the spiritual aspect of mermaids, plus their role as symbols of female sexuality and the sacred feminine.

Mermaids Online

weekiwachee.com/mermaids
mahinamermaid.com
projectmermaids.com
mermaidtails.net

Mermaids on Screen

Mermaids (2017) Documentary about real folk living the merfolk life, looking at what drives us to don tails and get with the finning and swimming. Not to be confused with the 1990 *Mermaids*, which stars Cher and Winona Ryder and is jolly good, but is not about mermaids in any way.

Mako Mermaids (2013 onwards) Spinoff of the popular H2O series, with more mermaid mishaps as the original mermaid trio deal with the consequences of a young boy falling into their magic pool and becoming a merman.

Mermaid Games

There are almost as many mermaid games for phones and tablets out there as there are fish in the sea – just trawl the app store. If you're feeling more traditional though, there are board games like the co-operative 'Mermaid Island' (available on Amazon), where your team of mermaids has to fend off a sea witch. Or for something *really* old school, there are still some original *Little Mermaid* board games around on eBay, for the true Ariel fan.

ACKNOWLEDGMENTS

Author Biographies

RUSS THORNE (author) is a freelance journalist who contributes to print titles including the *Independent*, *I* and the *London Evening Standard* along with various magazines and websites. His previous books include *The Magical History of Unicorns*, and titles exploring fantasy art, tattoos, zombies, vampires and the Day of the Dead.

TERA LYNN CHILDS (foreword) is the RITA-award-winning young adult author of the mythology-based *Oh. My. Gods.* series, the *Forgive My Fins* mermaid romance series, the kick-butt monster-hunting *Sweet Venom* trilogy, and the *Darkly Fae* series. She also wrote the *City Chicks* sweet chick lit romance series and co-wrote the *Hero Agenda* and *Creative HeArts* series. Tera lives nowhere in particular and spends her time writing wherever she can find a comfy chair and a steady stream of caffeinated beverages.

Picture Credits

Special thanks to all the artists who have contributed artwork to this book, in page order: © **Selina Fenech** 1c & 72 & 74, 3 & 58 & 63, 46 & 49, 47, 48, 50, 51, 52 & 54 & 128, 53, 55, 57, 60, 61, 62, 64, 65, 66, 67, 68, 69 & 75, 71, 73, 76 & 83, 77, 78, 81, 82, 84, 87 & 90, 88; © **Pat Brennan** 2 & 104r & 105, 104l; © **Jasmine Becket-Griffith; www.strangeling.com** 4, 10, 11, 13, 14, 20, 21, 22–23, 24, 26, 38, 39, 40, 41; © **Josephine Wall** 5b & 34 & 35l, 29, 30 & 31, 32 & 33; © **Patricia MacCarthy** 5t & 95 & 103 & 124t; © **Camilla Ceccatelli** 6t; **By Marta Nael/© Ediciones Babylon** 6b & 18–19; © **Olivia Rose** 7, 25, 44; © **Ana Cruz** 8t; © **Sergey Sezonov** 9; © **ElXi-Ameyn** 15; © **Max Wan** 16 & 17; © **Joana Shino** 28; © **Cris Ortega** 36–37 & back cover; © **Laura Csajagi** 42–43, 45; © **Jonas Joedicke** 59; © **Lindsey Look** 86 & 89; © **Ginger Kelly Studio, Lauren Kelly Small; www.artbygingerkelly.com** 91, 101, 102; © **Rebecca Sinz** 92 & 96, 93 & 100, 107, 109, 108; © **Nazar Noschenko** 94 & 99; © **Natalia Hlebnicova; tigress0787.deviantart.com** 97, 98; © **Senyphine** 112, and courtesy of Editions Le Héron d'Argent 110–11 & 124b; © **2018 George Patsouras** 106; © **Sutat Palama** 113, 114; © **Milica Jevtic (MilyKnight)** 119; © **Ksenia Kim (goldkanet)** 117, 121; © **Malwina 'merkerinn' Kwiatkowska** 118; © **Samrae Duke** 120; © **Tiffany Toland-Scott** 122 & front cover, 123, 125, 126.

Courtesy of **Shutterstock.com** and the following artists: Svesla Tasla 1l/r & 3l/r & 128l/r; Atelier Sommerland 35r; AlenaLazareva 56; Ellerslie 115. Courtesy of **Bridgeman Images**: Hardy, E.S. (19th century)/Private Collection 79 & 85. Courtesy of/© **Grace Page/Hire A Mermaid UK** 116.